Ned Glasier, Emily Lim
and Company Three

BRAINSTORM

The Original Playscript
And a Blueprint for
Creating Your Own Production

Foreword by Professor Sarah-Jayne Blakemore

NICK HERN BOOKS

London

www.nickhernbooks.co.uk

A Nick Hern Book

Brainstorm first published in Great Britain in 2016 as a paperback original by Nick Hern Books Limited, The Glasshouse, 49a Goldhawk Road, London W12 8QP, in association with Company Three

Brainstorm copyright © 2016 Ned Glasier, Emily Lim and Company Three Foreword copyright © 2016 Sarah-Jayne Blakemore

Ned Glasier, Emily Lim and Company Three have asserted their right to be identified as the authors of this work

Cover image: Matt Hodges

Designed and typeset by Nick Hern Books, London Printed in the UK by CPI Books (UK) Ltd

A CIP catalogue record for this book is available from the British Library

ISBN 978 1 84842 587 3

See page 71 for more information about staging your own production of *Brainstorm*, incorporating the scientific content featured in the script, and how to develop your own personal content.

Contents

For Antione,
who inspired the idea in the first place

Foreword

In 2013, I first saw *Brainstorm* as a scratch performance by twenty-five teenage members of Company Three (then Islington Community Theatre). The group, together with directors Ned Glasier and Emily Lim, had seen my TED Talk on the teenage brain and been inspired to create a play about what was happening inside their heads. Ned and Emily approached me and my former PhD student, Dr Kate Mills, to talk to them about the science of the adolescent brain.

When I saw the scratch performance, I had no idea what to expect, but from the first scene onwards I was mesmerised by the imaginative interpretation of the science and the brilliant performances by the talented young people. The play was innovative and clever, and incredibly poignant, telling the stories of the complex relationships between the young people and their parents, set within the context of the science of how the adolescent brain develops.

I wanted to get more involved and was delighted that a grant from the Wellcome Trust enabled Kate and me to spend more time with the directors and young people to develop the play. Our first step on this journey was a twenty-minute performance and talk by the young people and myself in front of four thousand people at the *Discovering the Future of Medicine* event at the Royal Albert Hall in London.

It is important that we find new ways to communicate our scientific discoveries to young people and the general public, and *Brainstorm* is a perfect example of this. The impact of the play on its audiences at the Royal Albert Hall, Park Theatre, National Theatre and on BBC iPlayer has been profound and long-lasting. The cast have told Kate and me stories of parents rethinking how they understand and interact with their children as a consequence of learning about brain development from the play. We have heard about headteachers who have seen the play and returned to their schools determined to do things differently.

And we have learned from the experience too. It's fascinating and important to learn about how the science of the adolescent brain is interpreted by young people themselves. We learn about their experiences, what's important to them and what they care about, and this gives us ideas for our next experiments.

It has always been important to me that science is accessible and that everyone has a role to play in communicating it, questioning it and sharing it. I hope this book enables many other young people to have the same experience of self-discovery that the cast of Company Three's *Brainstorm* did, and that many more audience members might start to understand the extraordinary potential of the teenage brain.

Sarah-Jayne Blakemore
Professor of Cognitive Neuroscience
UCL Institute of Cognitive Neuroscience

About *Brainstorm*

Brainstorm was created by Ned Glasier, Emily Lim and the company:

Michael Adewale, Doyin Ajiboye, Sama Aunallah, Yaamin Chowdhury, Jack Hughes, Noah Landoni, Dylan Lubo, Gracia Kayindo, Romeo Mika, Kassius Nelson, Tyrel Phan, Serafina Willow and Segen Yosife.

Directors	Ned Glasier and Emily Lim
Designer	Charlie Damigos
Lighting Designer	Jo Town
Sound Designer	Elena Peña
Movement Director	Daragh O'Leary
Consultant	Professor Sarah-Jayne Blakemore
Neuroscientists	and Dr Kate Mills
Producer	Adam Coleman
Company Stage Manager	Sarah Stott

Members of Company Three who contributed to the early development of *Brainstorm*: Jahmai Allen, Samia Amao, Stanley Amisah-Andoh, Antione Azille, Kiki Bowen, Larissa Fonseca, Chelsea Green, KJ Gomez-Danso, Eliza Greenslade, Helawit Hailemariam, Sam Head, James Jani, Anisha Maxin Ngagba, Jéssica Noque, Kofi Odoom, Angie Peña Arenas, Corey Peterson, Jonathan Pontes-Betu, Olga Popiolek-Szulczewska, Tom Proctor, Pia Richards-Glöckner, Megan Saunders, Soumia Sebbar, Georgie Stevens, Josh Shanny-Wynter and Roxlyne Quaye.

A scratch version of *Brainstorm* was performed at Platform Islington in March 2013. This published version of the show was first performed at Park Theatre, London, in January 2015, then at the National Theatre in July 2015 and April 2016. *Brainstorm* was adapted for BBC iPlayer in November 2015 as part of BBC's *Live from Television Centre*, produced in partnership with Battersea Arts Centre and Arts Council England.

An archive film recording of the July 2015 production of *Brainstorm* is held at the National Theatre Archive and is accessible by appointment. For further information, please visit www.nationaltheatre.org.uk.

About Company Three

'Captures the hormonal rush and wild mood swings of teenage existence… exhilarating' *Guardian* on *Brainstorm*

Company Three creates a space in which young people can speak to adults, and in which adults will really listen.

Originally formed as Islington Community Theatre in 2008, we work with a company of young people aged 11–19, all referred or nominated by teachers and youth workers as those most likely to benefit from our work.

Our plays are part of an ongoing exploration about what it means to be a teenager, created through long-term collaboration between our members and professional theatremakers.

We run regular training courses in devising theatre with young people for teachers, directors, playwrights and practitioners.

www.companythree.co.uk

Acknowledgements

Company Three would like to thank Lyndsey Turner, Ben Power, Fran Miller and everyone at the National Theatre and the National Theatre Studio; Jez Bond and the team at Park Theatre; Jonathan Gibbs, Laura Campbell and everyone at Platform Islington; Jayne Gold and her Year 8 students at Elizabeth Garret Anderson School; current and former Trustees of Company Three; Izzy Madgwick; Robert Blakey; Angie Peña Arenas; Mattia Pagura; Guy Jones; Kwami Odoom; Jonathan Samuels; Camilla Greenwell; Fergus Dingle; Ruth Little; Jack Lowe; Beck Smith; Professor Vincent Walsh; Gary Horner; Salvador Bettencourt Avila; Will Oates and Ella Macfadyen.

Thanks to the Dame Alice Owen Foundation, Tuixen Foundation, Cripplegate Foundation and Sumners Foundation for their continued and long-standing support of Company Three's work. Thanks also to the Shanly Foundation and all the individuals who have supported our work on *Brainstorm* over the past years.

Special thanks to the Wellcome Trust, who have been the principal funder of the development of *Brainstorm*.

Finally, extra special thanks to all the parents of the cast, without whose support *Brainstorm* would not have been possible.

BRAINSTORM

The Original Playscript

This is the version of the script performed at the National Theatre, London, in July 2015. It was performed by:

Michael Adewale
Doyin Ajiboye
Sama Aunallah
Yaamin Chowdhury
Jack Hughes
Noah Landoni
Gracia Kayindo
Tyrel Phan
Serafina Willow
Segen Yosife

A Note on the Play

The play is performed on a simple white stage, surrounded
by plain wooden furniture: drawers, cabinets, bedside tables,
a large wardrobe and a bed with a white duvet cover and pillows.

Cables from the theatre hang from above, linked to white
four-way plug adaptors that seem to connect to the back of the
set. Music plays from a mobile phone connected to a portable
speaker on one of the cabinets.

There are two microphones – one upstage, one downstage.
Whenever the microphones are used during the play it indicates
that a parent is talking.

There is a bedroom lamp onstage at the start. Other lamps
emerge from the drawers during the play. These are used to
indicate individual bedrooms during the Bedrooms and
Sprouting scenes and for the Brain Scan scene, where they are
anonymously lit to provide answers to a series of questions.

As the cast arrive onstage they use their mobile phones to
communicate with each other using WhatsApp. At various
points in the play they project their phones on to the wardrobe,
revealing their screens to the audience.

During the play the cast talk openly to the audience and stage
manager.

A forward slash (/) in the text indicates an interruption.

Before the Show

As the audience arrive they are given cards on which they are asked to write a message to their teenage self, starting with the words 'You don't know this yet but…'

These are collected as the audience enter the theatre and some are selected to be read out in the final scene of the play.

Introduction

GRACIA *walks on stage. She speaks to the audience.*

GRACIA   Hello.

So.

JACK *enters. He sits down and takes out his phone. Throughout the scene, whenever someone enters, they take out their phone and sit sending messages to each other via a central WhatsApp group, commenting on how they're feeling, what's happening in the show, and the audience.*

That's Jack.

(*To the audience.*) Look at him.

What do you think of him?

Do you like him?

What do you think is going on in his head, right now?

Jack's thirteen. He's the youngest one here. He hates that. Don't you, Jack?

Jack used to live in Singapore, but now he lives in Finsbury Park.

When we first did this play in January he had quite a high voice, but now it's getting really deep.

Say something, Jack.

JACK *doesn't say anything.*

Say something.

JACK *says whatever pops into his head.*

GRACIA   Say something longer.

JACK   No.

GRACIA   Look at his little face.

SERAFINA *enters*.

That's Serafina.
Serafina's fourteen.

Serafina once locked herself in her room for
a whole week and only spoke to her mum by
text message.

She's got this type of epilepsy – so she might like
have a seizure for a few seconds or something
during the show… so, yeah.

Oh, and she is totally in love with Benedict
Cumberbatch.

SERAFINA   He has this eye thing, like one eye is a different
colour to the other eye.

NOAH *enters*.

GRACIA   This is Noah. He's fifteen.

NOAH   Hi. Hello.

GRACIA   Noah hates sitting still.

Last year he broke into a construction site and
hung off the scaffolding on the third floor – cos
he's an idiot.

MICHAEL *enters*.

That's Michael.
He's fifteen too.

Whenever Michael does anything stupid, his mum
tells him she's going to send him back to Nigeria
to live in a village with no shoes.

MICHAEL   (*To an audience member.*) She never does though.

GRACIA   This is a play about us.
It's about our brains.
And it's about you.

Twenty years ago scientists thought that teenage
brains were the same as adult brains, but like
really rubbish versions of them.

Scientists thought teenagers were just crap adults.

Most people thought teenagers were just crap adults.

In fact, most people still do.

TYREL *enters*.

This is Tyrel. He's sixteen.

So then scientists started using these machines
called MRI machines to scan people's brains and
they learned loads more about them.

And they found out that teenagers aren't actually
crap adults.

They found out that our brains are different to
adult brains and that that's okay, that's a good
thing, they're meant to be like that.

Beat.

Tyrel does this wicked impression of a caterpillar.

Do it, Tyrel.

TYREL   Shut up.

MICHAEL   Do it.

TYREL   I'm not doing it.

GRACIA   And so scientists now know that teenage brains are
different for a reason, but if you go and ask people
in the street or teachers or bus drivers or politicians
or parents or the security guards that follow us
around in shops, I bet they don't know that.

We know. And we think you should know.

SAMA and DOYIN *enter.*

That's Sama.

And that's Doyin.

They're both sixteen.

Doyin's like really clever, she won this speech competition and she's Head Girl and she's Nigerian, like Michael, and she's a really good singer.

Sama has thousands of followers on Twitter, but they're all One Direction fans so they don't count.

She's really good at doing her make-up. She hasn't left the house without make-up on since she was eleven.

In Sama's brain there are eighty-six billion neurons.

A neuron is a cell that sends information.

In your brain, and your brain, and your brain right now, there are eighty-six billion neurons.

Everyone has eighty-six billion neurons.

Even Michael does.

In Serafina's brain, right now, there are neurons sending loads of information about Benedict Cumberbatch's eyes.

Whenever you think of something, or do something, or look at your phone, or dance to some sick tune, or think about someone really fit –

SERAFINA   Like Benedict Cumberbatch.

GRACIA   Whenever you do *anything* your neurons get connected up.

They get connected up by these things called synapses.

YAAMIN *enters.*

That's Yaamin. Yaamin's sixteen.

He's trying to grow facial hair but it's not really working out for him.

He once had a massive fight with his mum because he bought the wrong kind of chicken from the supermarket.

YAAMIN   (*To an audience member.*) It was just a fucking chicken.

GRACIA   And what scientists know now is that by the time you start puberty –

NOAH   Like Jack.

    JACK *looks up.*

GRACIA   By the time you're like Jack –

    There are some parts of your brain that have way too many connections – loads and loads and loads of synapses.

    You've grown all these connections – it's called sprouting – and your brain is like really messy.

    When you become a teenager you've got more connections in some parts of your brain than you'll ever have again.

    SEGEN *enters.*

    This is Segen.

    Segen's going to be seventeen next week.

    She met her dad for the first time like a year ago.

    She's genuinely worried she might be addicted to her mobile phone.

    I'm Gracia. I'm eighteen. I'm the oldest one here.

    They are all still on their phones.

    Look at us.

What do you think of us?

What do you think we're thinking about right now?

Beat.

Do you want to see?

Pause. Clicks and notifications. GRACIA *is on her phone for a moment.*

This is WhatsApp.

Her phone screen appears on the wardrobe behind her.

It's a messaging app.

It's like texting, but it's free.
And our parents aren't on it so it's better.

Since the play started we've sent all these messages to each other.

She scrolls back through the messages the cast have sent one another since the beginning of the show. As we read them, the cast continue to send messages to the group.

GRACIA *puts her phone away.*

Look at us.

Think of all them billions of neurons in your brain.

All those connections you're making while you're looking at us.

It looks like lightning and it sounds like the fastest typing in the world.

Like machine guns.

They look up from their phones.

Look at us.

Who's your favourite?

Who would you sit next to on the bus?

Who would you have been friends with when you were our age?

Who's always in trouble?

Who is in love?

Who do you think tells their parents to *fuck off*?

Who spends the most time locked away in their room?

Look at us.

Look at us.

Look at us.

Beat.

DOYIN *stands. The others run to a drawer or a cupboard.*

DOYIN   Imagine you could open a door in our heads and look right inside our brains.

Everyone opens their drawer.

Imagine you could see all the connections we've been sprouting ever since we were born.

All lying around like wires and clothes and a whole load of crap on the floor.

SEGEN *empties a drawer of clothes and objects all over the stage.*

It's a mess. A total mess.

DOYIN *starts playing music through a speaker.*

SAMA *plays* DOYIN*'s mum.*

SAMA   DOYIN!

DOYIN   YES, MUM?

SAMA   WHERE ARE YOU?

DOYIN   I'M IN MY ROOM.

DOYIN *turns the speaker up a notch.*

SAMA   DOYIN!

DOYIN   WHAT?

DOYIN *turns the speaker up a notch again.*

SAMA   WHAT'S GOING ON IN THERE?

DOYIN   NOTHING

DOYIN *turns the speaker up and up and up and up to drown out her mum.*

SAMA   DOYIN!

DOYIN   I'M BUSY!

As the music gets louder and louder, the cast explode their bedrooms, pulling objects and clothes out of the drawers and cupboards and making a massive mess.

Bedrooms

The cast are in their bedrooms.

YAAMIN *plays* SERAFINA*'s mum.*

YAAMIN   SERAFINA! TURN IT DOWN!

SERAFINA My brain is like my bedroom.
          It's a mess, a total mess.
          It's got everything in it.

YAAMIN   SERAFINA!

SERAFINA Cardboard boxes. Bedding all over the floor. Three
          Build-A-Bears. Forty Blue Nose Bears. Seven
          snow globes. Homework. Bedding. A massive dog
          cage that I can't even get out of the door.

YAAMIN   SERAFINA!

SERAFINA WHAT?!

          Sherlock has this mind palace where he keeps all
          his information and facts and evidence and stuff
          all neat and tidy.

          I tried to make my brain into a mind palace once.
          It's basically physically impossible.

JACK   I *hate* tidying.
          Why should I? It's my room.

          My parents think it's all crap, but I'm like, I don't
          know what I'll need so I'm going to keep it and
          I can't put it away anyway because my mum and
          dad take up half my wardrobe with their clothes.

          He opens the wardrobe to show us.

          Look. It's so annoying.

          There's stuff all over the floor, stuff on the walls.
          A massive tub of bouncy balls I've been collecting
          my whole life. (*To an audience member.*) Do you
          want one?

There's a pirate treasure map my dad made me.
It's got swirly glitter bits instead of crosses.

SEGEN   The first shelf contains books I stole from school.
The second shelf contains books I own from school.
The third shelf contains more books.
And the fourth shelf just contains shit.

SAMA   My wallpaper that I put up. Loads of candles.
A dreamcatcher. Cushions. Photos of my friends.
Photos of Harry Styles. My make-up. More make-up. Two guitars. Folders. And my teddy bear.

NOAH   Yeah, so.

Clothes and like a lot of stuff.

Amp. Not plugged in yet.

Speaker. Not plugged in yet.

Printer. Not plugged in yet.

Some other stuff… errr… just clothes.

I never really dealt with what happened with my dad. I just put it under the bed with a whole load of other stuff.

All my books.

Birdcage.

More stuff.

Elvis.

Bob Marley.

Light.

That's it really.

DOYIN   I move my room around every three weeks. I just get bored and I move the furniture around, like I'll put the bed under the window… I'll move the drawers over there… the cupboard goes there… then three weeks later I'll change it again.

There's a hole in the wall behind my door when
I slammed it so hard cos I did *not* want to wash
the dishes.

JACK   My room's messy but it means I've got everything.
My brain's messy but it means I've got everything.

The connections I've been forming for my whole
life are all still there. I haven't lost anything
important, it just takes a long time to find anything.

SEGEN *plays* JACK*'s mum.*

SEGEN   JACK!

JACK   I'M DOING IT!

TYREL   My brain is like my bedroom. I don't want my
parents anywhere near it. I don't want them
coming in all the time.

Except I don't have a door on my door.
They pulled it off because I used to lock my
brother out.

I got home and I was like

WHERE'S MY DOOR?

GRACIA   I sleep on the top bunk and my little sister sleeps
on the bottom. My auntie used to sleep there too,
but she went back to France so now we have it all
to ourselves.

YAAMIN   Our room is next to our mum's room.

Every morning I go in and she's sleeping and I kiss
her on the forehead and I kiss my baby sister on the
forehead and I go to college.

In Islam it goes Allah Mother Mother Mother
Father.

That's about right, I think.

SAMA *plays* YAAMIN*'s mum.*

SAMA   YAAMIN!

YAAMIN   YEAH?

MUM   CAN YOU GO TO THE SHOP FOR ME?

YAAMIN   OKAY!

TYREL   I have three hiding places.

            One has money in it.

            One has photos of my mum and dad when they
            were babies.

            One has… Nah man I'm not telling you that one.

            Seriously I'm not telling you.

MICHAEL   I have a computer desktop table… with no
            computer on it. My dad took my computer away.
            He just came in and took it. I was so mad. He said
            my bedroom was like my office because I was in
            there playing games for like eight hours every day.

            I had this massive cup of water so I never even
            had to leave my room to go to the kitchen.

            My dad's got this properly sensible job – he – he
            works in the civic centre. He's like a housing
            officer or something but I don't know really know
            what that means.

            This one time, my dad's laundry got mixed up with
            mine. He wears this massive white shirt and I found
            it in my room and wore it to school by mistake.

            I looked like a right muppet.

SEGEN   Basically, if I'm in my room, I'm on my phone.

            I'm always on my phone.

            You can learn so much on your phone. Like
            YouTube, Wikipedia, Wiki-Answers, Urban
            Dictionary, Snapchat.

            And I can store it all too. It's like my own library.

If you go to my notepad – I'm not showing you it,
it's private – just the titles of the folders. I'm not
telling you no more.

It's got …

It's got a French song.

Chapters from the Bible that I remember when
I'm feeling low.

It's got directions to somewhere. Don't know where.

A-level help.

My best conversations from WhatsApp.

All the boys I've ever kissed.

And… all my YouTube tutorials that I've saved.

YAAMIN *plays* SEGEN*'s mum.*

YAAMIN   SEGEN!

SEGEN   If I hear my mum coming, I throw my phone
across the room and lie on my bed with my books
like I'm doing homework. I don't have a desk
because that's boring.

YAAMIN   SEGEN!

SEGEN   WHAT?

YAAMIN   CAN I COME IN?
I'VE GOT YOUR WASHING.

SEGEN   LEAVE IT OUTSIDE.

YAAMIN   ARE YOU DOING YOUR HOMEWORK?

SEGEN   YES.

YAAMIN   I KNOW YOU WERE ON YOUR PHONE.

SEGEN   I WAS DOING MY HOMEWORK ON
MY PHONE.

Sprouting

TYREL *is filming himself on his phone. His face appears projected on the wardrobe.*

TYREL   Hello.

               Welcome to my YouTube tutorial.

               This week I'm showing you how to play Two Dot.

               He opens the game app Two Dot on his phone. It appears on the wardrobe.

               Hold on. Let me just get the music on.
               It's really sick.

               The music starts.

               There we go.

               This is Two Dot.

               It's really simple.

               Connect the dots to win a point.

               The more connections you make. The more points you win.

               He starts playing the game, connecting dots and winning points. DOYIN *watches.*

DOYIN   My brain is always making new connections.

               Every time I go on YouTube and watch a new tutorial, the neurons in my brain get connected up again and again by synapses.

               She looks at the wardrobe. TYREL *wins another point.*

               Like that.

               The rest of the cast start to film themselves on their phones, holding their screens towards the audience.

SAMA   In this video I'm going to teach you to apply make-up.

GRACIA   I'm going to show you how to use a henna cone.

YAAMIN   To solve a Rubik's Cube.

JACK   To throw really straight.

SEGEN   To text really fast.

SERAFINA   To find all the bobby pins you've ever lost down the back of your drawers.

NOAH   To play 'Dirty Old Town' by The Pogues on the harmonica.

MICHAEL   To beat everyone at FIFA.

            The cast film DOYIN *as she talks.*

DOYIN   Imagine you could open a door in my head and see what happens every time I learn something new.

            Because I swear down right now it feels like I do something new every single day. Like learning a new song or making a film or buying new make-up or finding that place on White Hart Lane that sells the best chips I've ever tasted –

            Chips are so buff.

            You'd see a whole load of my neurons getting connected up in a way they never have before.

            And every time I do the same thing, the same connections happen.

            Again and again.

            The cast ask a nearby audience member to film them using their phone.

SAMA   Apply concealer under eyes and on spots.
            Fill in eyebrows.
            Prime eyelids.

GRACIA   Hold the cone from the top and squeeze it with your thumb.

YAAMIN   Apply a number of algorithms – R is the right side of the cube, L is the left side, U in the top, D is the bottom and B is the back.

JACK   Keep your arm straight, align, take your time.

SEGEN   Put your thumbs either side of the space bar, equal distance to the letters.

SERAFINA   Find a magnet from your fridge. Tie it on to a pen, like a fishing line. Dangle it down the back of your drawers so the bobby pins stick to it.

            NOAH *plays the first line of 'Dirty Old Town' on his harmonica.*

TYREL   When you've connected all the dots, you go up a level.

MICHAEL   X to pass, square to shoot, circle to volley.

            They take back their phones and film DOYIN *again.*

DOYIN   The more I use those connections, the stronger they get. That's why you get better at things the more you do them.

            Like singing. Or Rubik's Cube. Or make-up. Or whatever.

            The connections you use all the time get stronger and stronger.

            And the connections you don't use – as you get older they start to die off.

            That's called pruning.

            It's a bit like tidying your room, when you throw away all the stuff you don't use any more. It basically means your brain gets better at doing certain things, but it's like a compromise because you lose loads of connections that you'll never get back.

It doesn't happen overnight. It takes years and years.

It's not like you wake up one day and you just get an adult brain.

It's not like when you get your period and you're like whoa I am a woman now.

That's important.

And it happens in different parts of your brain at different times.

That's really important.

Right now I've got more connections in some parts of my brain than I'll ever have again.

I wish my mum could see that.

JACK *plays* MICHAEL*'s dad.*

JACK MICHAEL!

MICHAEL YES, DAD?

JACK HAVE YOU SEEN MY SHIRT?

MICHAEL WHAT?

JACK MY SHIRT! I'M LATE FOR WORK.

MICHAEL I DON'T HAVE YOUR SHIRT.

JACK ARE YOU SURE? CAN I JUST COME IN AND LOOK?

MICHAEL NO, DAD, I HAVEN'T GOT IT, WHY WOULD I HAVE YOUR STUPID SHIR…

He finds the shirt screwed up on the floor and picks it up.

Oh shit.

MICHAEL *looks at the shirt.*

Pre-Frontal Cortex

SAMA *looks at* MICHAEL *holding the shirt.*

SAMA   There's this bit at the front of the brain called the Pre-Frontal Cortex.

It's right here, right in the front of your brain.

It's the bit that controls your planning and consequences and stuff like that.

It's the really sensible bit. It's the bit that stops you doing stupid stuff. The bit that says 'Don't do that, or that will happen.'

It's a bit like your dad.

MICHAEL *looks at the shirt. He looks at the others. They each find a piece of their parents' clothing somewhere in the space. They put the item of clothing on, carefully.*

Sudden shift. The cast become their parents. It's like they're caught in the spotlight.

JACK *speaks into the microphone. He passes it down the line.*

JACK   Alright, my name is Alex. I have a son called Jack, he's nearly as tall as me. I like to DJ at parties.

YAAMIN   Hi, I'm Rana. I'm Yaamin's mum. I have a seven-month-old baby named Zara. I like watching Indian programmes.

DOYIN   Hello. My name is Rachel I am Doyin's mother. I used to be Head Girl in my senior year, like Doyin is now. I am proud of her but she needs to work harder.

SEGEN   Hello, I'm Sofia, Segen's mum. I work at Harringay Primary school and I love shoes.

NOAH   Hi, I'm Amber, Noah's mum. I like *EastEnders* and cooking.

MICHAEL   Hello. I'm Mr Adewale. I'm Michael's father. I'm a housing officer.

SERAFINA   Hi, I'm OJ, Serafina's mum. My favourite colour is purple, so I actually died my hair purple.

TYREL   Hi I'm Ricky, I'm Tyrel's dad and I'm a construction worker.

SAMA   Hi I'm Tarek, Sama's dad. And in my spare time I write poetry. I share it on Facebook, I get quite a lot of likes. I actually have more Facebook friends than my daughters put together.

GRACIA   Hi I'm Ndaya, I'm Gracia's mother. I like watching Nollywood films and eating fufu at the same time.

SAMA   I studied at Oxford University, I studied English. And that's where Sama's going to go.

TYREL   I love to dance at weddings. When the music comes on I just can't help myself.

            'All Night Long' by Lionel Ritchie starts to play in the background.

            TYREL *starts dancing like his dad. Someone opens a disco-ball app on their phone. It appears on the wardrobe. One by one the parents start to join in, tentatively at first.*

SERAFINA   I'm a Maths and English teacher. Serafina was home-schooled for a year and I was her teacher.

MICHAEL   (*To an audience member.*) Is Michael being bad? Can you tell me?

NOAH   I can always tell when Noah is lying.

SEGEN   I like expensive wine.

DOYIN   I love to pray, glory be to God, and listening to Fela Kuti.

YAAMIN   I'm a social worker and a driving instructor. I'm giving my son free lessons but if he doesn't start getting up in the morning he's going to have to pay for them himself.

JACK   I like to take pictures of graffiti.

The music takes over. The parents let loose on the dance floor.

After a while, MICHAEL, *still playing his dad, looks at his watch and stops the party.*

MICHAEL   Hello DJ, DJ?

The music stops.

I'm sorry I would like to party all night long, but I have to go to work in the morning.

The parents nod. The cast take off their parents' clothes and watch MICHAEL.

He speaks to the audience.

I'm a housing officer.

I work in the civic centre and we are part of the council.

Is there anything you need, anything I can help you get, anything I can help you with?

I'm part of the housing service and I can help you with referrals, housing, things like that.

Have you got any housing problems?

(*To an audience member.*) Can I ask –
Is Michael behaving himself?
He's being bad, isn't he?
You can tell me. Michael's mum would really like to know.

SAMA   The Pre-Frontal Cortex is one of the last bits of the teenage brain to develop.

DOYIN *steals the microphone from* MICHAEL. *He resists.*

It takes ages and ages to work properly.

DOYIN plays MICHAEL*'s mum.*

DOYIN   MICHAEL!

*Music. The cast scramble to tidy up their
bedrooms as best they can, shoving things
haphazardly in drawers, cupboards and under
the bed.*

MICHAEL   YES?

DOYIN   MICHAEL, OPEN THE DOOR.

MICHAEL   OKAY!

DOYIN   JACK!

JACK   DON'T COME IN!

DOYIN   SERAFINA!

SERAFINA OKAY!

DOYIN   SEGEN! CAN I COME IN?

SEGEN   WAIT A MINUTE.

DOYIN   NOAH!

NOAH   YES!

DOYIN   YAAMIN, OPEN THE DOOR.

YAAMIN   I'M COMING!

DOYIN   TYREL! HAVE YOU TIDIED UP?!

TYREL   I'M DOING IT!

DOYIN   SAMA! UNLOCK THE DOOR!

SAMA   ALRIGHT!

DOYIN   I'M COMING IN, GRACIA!

GRACIA   OKAY!

DOYIN   MICHAEL!
                   AM I TALKIN' TO SOMEONE?
                   WHO BORN WHO?

ALL YOU KNOW HOW TO DO IS PLAY
YOUR PLAYSTATION
GAME GAME GAME GAME EVERY DAY
IDIOT!
OMO LONDON SHA!
OH MY GOD THIS BOY WANNA GIVE ME
HEART ATTACK!
BURUKU!
AT YOUR AGE?
I DON'T WASH PLATES BECAUSE I CAN'T
WASH IT!
IF YOU DON'T COME DOWN AND WASH
THE PLATE I WILL PUT IT ON MY HEAD!
IF I WAS NOT HERE, WHAT WOULD YOU
DO?
ARE YOU MAD?

BEFORE I OPEN MY EYES YOU HAD
BETTER OPEN THIS DOOR!

MICHAEL! YOU HAVE THREE SECONDS –
THREE… TWO…

OKAY MAYBE FIVE

FIVE… FOUR… THREE

I'M COMING IN NOW!
WHAT IS GOING ON IN THERE?
OPEN THE DOOR! MICHAEL! MICHAEL!

Parent Duologues

The music stops. The cast stop tidying.

One by one the parents enter the bedrooms to confront their children.

DOYIN *plays* MICHAEL*'s mum.*

DOYIN   MICHAEL!
           Is that your dad's shirt?

MICHAEL   No…

DOYIN   It is. It's way too big for you.

MICHAEL   I didn't realise – I –

DOYIN   He's been looking for it everywhere.
           Michael, it is filthy.
           What are you thinking of, eh?

MICHAEL   I was –

DOYIN   Are you stupid?

MICHAEL   No.

DOYIN   You tell me you're mature but you act like this.
           You want your own keys to the house but you're
           still a child.

           Go and mop the floor.

MICHAEL   I ain't mopping nothing I hate mopping.

DOYIN   I WILL SEND YOU TO NIGERIA, I WILL
           SEND YOU TO THE VILLAGE WITH NO
           SHOES –

MICHAEL   Mum, I…

MUM   GO AND MOP THE FLOOR.

           ***

           GRACIA *plays* JACK*'s mum.*

GRACIA   It's not working.

JACK   That's the wrong one.

GRACIA   Wrong what?

JACK   The wrong remote.

GRACIA   Why didn't you tell me?

JACK   *I did.*

GRACIA   What button is it?

JACK   Source. Like I said. Mum, I'm busy you / know.

GRACIA   Source?

JACK   Yes.

GRACIA   There isn't a source button.

JACK   It's the one that says TV on it.

GRACIA   TV?

JACK   Yes.

GRACIA   Why didn't you say TV?

JACK   Because it's the source button.

GRACIA   How would I know that?

JACK   Everyone knows that.
              Can you shut the door please?

              ***

              YAAMIN *plays* SAMA*'s dad.*

YAAMIN   How'd it go?

SAMA   Good.

YAAMIN   Did you get all the answers?

SAMA   Yeah

YAAMIN   A-star?

SAMA   Hope so.

YAAMIN   Well done.

SAMA   Yeah.

**

NOAH *plays* DOYIN*'s mum.*

NOAH   Am I so embarrassing to you?

DOYIN   I just don't want you to come.

NOAH   Why?

DOYIN   You'll be like 'Before we eat let's all say a prayer for Doyin's birthday.'

It's not like Nigeria you know.

NOAH   Prayer is important, Doyin.

DOYIN   I know.

NOAH   It's a special day for me too.

DOYIN   Why?

NOAH   It's your *birth*day.

DOYIN   EXACTLY.

NOAH   I was there you know.

DOYIN   It's my sixteenth.

Beat.

NOAH   I won't come if you don't want me to.

DOYIN   I don't.

**

SEGEN *plays* TYREL*'s mum.*

TYREL   Can I say… shit?

SEGEN   No.

TYREL   Can I say crap?

SEGEN   No.

TYREL   You're taking the piss.

SEGEN   Tyrel!

TYREL   Can I say bollocks?

SEGEN   No.

TYREL   Can I have my door back?

SEGEN   NO.

TYREL   For fuck's sake –

SEGEN   TYREL!

***

SERAFINA *is in the middle of a text conversation with her mum. Her phone screen appears on the wardrobe. The first five messages have already been sent. The rest of the conversation is texted live.*

MUM   *Where are you?*

SERAFINA *Where do you think?*

MUM   *Are you coming out?*

SERAFINA *No.*

MUM   *Why?*

SERAFINA (*Texting.*) You know why.

MUM   It's been a week.

SERAFINA I know.

MUM   Why won't you come out?

SERAFINA You know why.

***

TYREL *plays* GRACIA*'s mum.*

TYREL   What time?

GRACIA   Around about 4 a.m.?

TYREL   No.

GRACIA   3?

TYREL   No.

GRACIA   2?

TYREL   No.

GRACIA   1?

TYREL   No.

GRACIA   Midnight!

TYREL   FINE!

GRACIA   AGH!

***

JACK *plays* SEGEN*'s mum.*

JACK   I love you.

SEGEN   I know.

MUM   I said I love you.

SEGEN   I said, I know.

MUM   Why are you like this?

SEGEN   I just am.

Can you go now?

***

SAMA *plays* NOAH*'s mum.*

SAMA   Did you unfriend me?

NOAH   What?

SAMA   On Facebook.

NOAH   Are you stalking me?

SAMA   Why did you unfriend me, Noah?

NOAH   You're not my friend.

SAMA   You added me in the first place.

                    ***

          YAAMIN *is holding a plastic bag and an energy*
          drink. As the argument heats up he starts to shake
          the bottle out of frustration.

          SERAFINA *plays* YAAMIN's *mum.*

SERAFINA You should have known.

YAAMIN   How would I know?

SERAFINA Because I always get a whole one.

YAAMIN   But I never bought one before.

SERAFINA One chicken. I said buy *one* chicken.

YAAMIN   It is one chicken.

SERAFINA It's all cut up.

YAAMIN   How would I know?

SERAFINA You should just know.

YAAMIN   Well why you didn't tell me?

SERAFINA How could I when you won't even speak to me.

YAAMIN   I'm speaking to you now, of course I speak to you.

SERAFINA Not like you used to.
          You used to tell me everything and now –

YAAMIN   Now what?

SERAFINA You're a stranger.
          We don't talk to each other.
          You don't tell me anything
          I don't even know you any more.

YAAMIN *stands alone, shaking the bottle*
furiously. JACK *walks to him and takes it off him.*
Music. JACK *opens a trapdoor in the stage and*
pulls out a tangled set of switches on long cables.
He gives a switch to each member of the cast. The
Brain Scan begins.

Brain Scan

A series of statements are projected on to the wardrobe. The cast answer yes or no to each statement by turning their lamp on or off.

Hello
Welcome to your Brain Scan
It's just a few questions
Lamps on = yes
Lamps off = no
Ready?

I am a teenager
I live with both my parents
I eat too much fried chicken
I think I'm clever
I think I'm good looking
I lied to my parents today
I'm in love
I steal things from shops
I hate puberty

Just a few more…
I can't sleep when my mum's not home
I cried today
I'm out of control
I don't tell my mum I love her any more
I wish I didn't look like my dad
Sex scares me
I wish my skin was a different colour
I'm worried no one will ever fall in love with me
I want to be…
A chef
A politician
A lawyer
An actor
A parent

I can be anything I want to be
Lamps off

Limbic System

JACK *starts clearing up the wires and putting them away.*

JACK   There's this part of the brain called the Limbic System.

It's in the middle of the brain and it's made up of loads of different bits and… there's one part of it called the Reward Centre that makes you want to have fun.

NOAH is bored. He wanders over to the bed and starts texting the WhatsApp group on his phone. It appears on the wardrobe.

NOAH   (*Texting.*) BORED BORED BORED BORED.

NOAH starts taking pictures of himself. They appear on the wardrobe.

JACK   It's the bit of the brain that makes you do stuff you shouldn't.

When you're a teenager your Limbic System is really hypersensitive. It goes wild whenever you do something fun or exciting or risky.

NOAH recruits MICHAEL to try and make JACK laugh using a random object they find under the bed. JACK gets as far as he can through the following speech before giving in.

JACK   I actually did a project at school about this. Shall I show you?

He takes a folder from a shelf and shows us a diagram.

So this is the brain and it's divided into different parts, this is the diagram that I drew, um, it's… So basically the Limbic System is a complex system of nerves and networks in the brain, so that includes, er, the olfactory bulbs, hippocampus, amygdala, that's really important that's like the main bit and the bit that does rewards and stuff and then there's hold on I'll just read these out, there's the… the anterior thalamic nuclei, fornix, columns of fornix, mammillary body, septum pellucidum, habenular commissure, cingulate gyrus, parahippocampal gyrus, limbic cortex, and limbic midbrain areas…

Eventually JACK *gives in.*

For fuck's sake.

NOAH *calls out to the stage manager.*

NOAH   Sarah, can we put the lights on the audience please?

He films the audience, zooming in on different people. Their faces appear on the wardrobe. He starts to wander into the audience – it feels dangerous, like he might do or say anything. He chooses someone to speak to and walks up to them.

Hello.

How are you?

Are you enjoying the show?

Do you want to play a game?

You do, don't you?

He convinces them to play the game. If they refuse, he asks someone else. When someone agrees, the cast celebrate.

(*To the audience member.*) What's your name?

Hello, [Name].

NOAH *takes a selfie with the audience member. It appears on the wardrobe.*

Everybody, [Name] wants to play a game, so we're all going to play a game.

I'm going to need a microphone for this.

NOAH *gives the phone to* MICHAEL, *who films him*.

NOAH *grabs the microphone*.

Okay.

This game is called Never Have I Ever.

And we're all going to play it. Okay?

I want to find the person with the best Limbic System in the room.

Because you're all sitting there looking really sensible and like you've never done anything stupid, but I bet you have.

I bet [Name] has.

Basically. You're all going to stand up.

Not yet, I haven't told you to yet.

You're all going to stand up *in a minute when I say so*.

And we're going to say 'Never Have I Ever something something'. And we're going to say something we've *actually* done. And if you've done that thing too, then you have to stay standing up. But if you haven't done that thing, then you're out of the game and you have to sit down.

And you've got to be honest.

Okay, so we're going to do a test round. Just so everyone understands.

Could everyone stand up please.

First one... Never have I ever seen a play at the National Theatre.

So everyone should be standing up because you have all been to the National Theatre. You're *at* the National Theatre. So well done, you're still in the game!

Okay, so here's the next one... Never have I ever
fancied Benedict Cumberbatch.

So if you have ever fancied Benedict
Cumberbatch, stay standing. And if you haven't,
sit down – you're out of the game.

NOAH *checks with a member of the audience who
has sat down.*

Just checking – you've never fancied Benedict
Cumberbatch? Even a little bit?

*He checks with a member of the audience who is
still standing up.*

And you have fancied him? So you're still in
the game.

Okay, good!
So, if you've done it, stay standing up.
If you haven't, you're out of the game and you
have to sit down.

Does everyone get how to play the game?

Shall we play for real?

Can everyone stand up again please?

Sarah, can you put some music on?

Ready? Let's play!

*One by one, cast members come forward to say
'Never Have I Ever' statements. The other cast
members watch the audience play and cheer them
on. NOAH is at the centre of it all, eating and
handing out sweets.*

GRACIA   Never have I ever got really really drunk and done
something stupid.

So just checking, everyone sitting down has never
got really drunk and done something stupid? So
you're out of the game.

SEGEN   Never have I ever kissed someone I shouldn't
            have kissed.

TYREL   Never have I ever stayed out all night without my
            parents knowing.

DOYIN   Never have I ever had a massive crush on my
            teacher.

YAAMIN   Never have I ever done a poo outside.

SERAFINA   Never have I ever got a piercing that I wasn't
            allowed to get.

MICHAEL   Never have I ever been out in public in only my
            underwear.

JACK   Never have I ever run away from the police.

SAMA   Never have I ever crashed my parent's car.

            *When only a small number of audience members
            are left standing, a klaxon sounds.*

NOAH   Okay, everyone, we're down to just a few people
            and we need to find a winner so we're going to
            play SPIN THE BOTTLE.

            *They play spin the bottle to identify the winner.
            NOAH asks the winner's name and gets the cast
            and audience chanting it wildly. The cast give the
            winner prizes bought from the pound shop.
            YAAMIN pulls a confetti canon over their head.*

            SO!

            *The atmosphere changes. It feels dangerous.
            The cast hype themselves up with sweets and
            energy drinks. NOAH is wired.*

            THE LIMBIC SYSTEM.

            The Limbic System is the bit that gives you the
            kick out of taking risks.

            It's the bit that says
            Go try that! Now that!

Try that! Do that! Now!
NOW! NOW! NOW! NOW! NOW!

You've got a brain full of ideas.
And you're young.
And you're hot.
You are really fucking hot.

NOAH *starts pulling the others off the bed. They move around the space getting ready for the party.*

I DARE YOU to put me in that shopping trolley and push me down the hill.

I DARE YOU to sit in the middle of the road and stop all the cars.

I DARE YOU to break all the doors in the cinema toilets.

I DARE YOU.

DO IT!
DO IT!
DO IT!
DO IT!

And your Pre-Frontal Cortex is going…

NOAH *jumps on the bed. He holds the microphone up to the sky. The sound of wind.*

Helloooo?

Pre-Frontal Cortex?

Are you there?

Can you hear me?

Music starts to build.

DO IT!

TAKE THIS.
SMOKE THIS.
DRINK THIS.
LICK THAT.

DO IT!

COME ON, MAN.
YOU A PUSSY OR WHAT?

NAH, YOU A CHICKEN? YOU'RE NOT
GONNA DO IT.

YOU ARE SO BORING!

HIT ME. IN THE FACE. HIT ME.

GIVE ME MORE.
GIVE ME MORE.
GIVE ME MORE.
GIVE ME MORE.

SUGAR RUSH!

DO IT THEN…
DO I LOOK LIKE A GIVE A SHIT?
GONNA CALL YOUR MUM FIRST?

DO IT!

Music breaks.

A massive party: wild, chaotic, out of control.

The cast dance, fight with pillows, down energy drinks and throw marshmallows at each other. TYREL dances like a gorilla. MICHAEL hurls JACK's tub of bouncy balls all over the stage. SEGEN and NOAH wrestle on the bed. NOAH force-feeds everyone energy drink.

They start mocking YAAMIN about the chicken story. He gets increasingly aggravated and angry. He shakes a bottle of energy drink violently.

YAAMIN loses control. He opens the energy drink. It goes everywhere, soaking him.

Stand-off

The cast back off. They turn to the audience as YAAMIN *shouts, as if he is speaking for them as well.*

YAAMIN   You can't scream at me the minute I walk in
the door

It's just a chicken

It's not my fault. I didn't do it deliberately.

I don't mean to –

How I am meant to know you wanted a whole one?

Don't scream at me

Don't scream at me

I'm telling you I had enough

Seriously

Just stop screaming at me.

I can never have a civilised conversation with you

I've had enough of this

This is so little

It's so little

You're meant to be my mum

You can't be screaming at little things about me

I'm telling you

Don't laugh

Don't laugh it's not funny

You act like a child

I've had enough

I've had enough

I'VE HAD ENOUGH.

Everyone bolts for their rooms.

Silence.

Eventually JACK *moves to the microphone.*

JACK *plays* MICHAEL*'s mum.*

JACK (*Gently.*) Michael.

Michael, please.

MICHAEL *gets up slowly. He fetches a mop and bucket. He starts mopping the stage.*

DOYIN *starts singing 'Cups (You're Gonna Miss Me When I'm Gone)' by Lulu and the Lampshades.*

When DOYIN *comes to the end of her song,* SEGEN *stands.*

SEGEN What do you mean?

What do you mean why am I like this?

Because

Because something changed and I don't know what

Because something in me changed

Because my life feels boring

Because I like my friends more

Because I need some space

Because I don't care

Because you're getting in my way

Because I'm old enough.

Because I'm big enough.

Because I'm not you.

Because your way isn't the only way.

I don't know why.

Just because.

I just am.

I'm sorry.

Risks

SAMA *stands. She opens WhatsApp on her phone. The group chat from earlier appears on the wardrobe. The following lines are sent as messages to the group.*

SAMA   My brain isn't finished yet.
              My Limbic System is hyper.
              My Pre-Frontal Cortex isn't ready.
              But think of all the things you can do.
              If you've still got all those connections.
              And you don't have the part that says.
              'No, don't do that, that won't work.'

              Everyone starts sending messages.

JACK   Mozart was fourteen when he wrote all that stuff.

SEGEN   Mark Zuckerberg made Facebook when he was nineteen.

NOAH   FUCKING FACEBOOK!!

GRACIA   Malala is the same age as me.

SAMA   Yeah. We take risks.
              Loads of risks.

GRACIA   Going shopping on my own

DOYIN   Walking into a room of strangers

JACK   Putting my hand up in class

SEGEN   Going to Italy to meet my dad

SERAFINA   Asking a boy out.
              Then asking him out again.

MICHAEL   Choosing a subject my parents didn't want me to take

YAAMIN   Choosing to pray five times a day

NOAH   Applying for my own bank card

TYREL   Teaching myself to make cupcakes.

              SAMA *clicks the phone off. It disappears from the wardrobe.*

You Say to Me, I Say to You

YAAMIN *turns to look at the others. He picks up the microphone and takes it to the centre of the stage. He speaks into the microphone. The cast each take a stack of handwritten placards out of the drawers and sit holding them face down.*

YAAMIN   You say to me

Your brain is broken.
It's like an adult's brain, but it doesn't work properly.

It's like you're in a city you've never been to and you don't have a map and you don't know what you're doing.
And you keep taking the wrong turns.

You say
Listen to me.
Don't worry.
One day you'll be okay.
Probably.
Your brain will start working properly.
One day your brain will be just like mine
And then you'll be okay.

But until then:
You've got to try and be more… like me.

He moves the microphone out of the way and speaks without it.

I say to you
My brain isn't broken.
It's beautiful.

I'm in a city I've never been to and I see bright lights and new ideas and fear and opportunity and a thousand million roads all lit up and flashing.

I say
There are so many places to explore but you've forgotten that they exist because every day you

walk the same way with your hands in your
pockets and your eyes on the floor.

I say
When I'm wild and out of control
It's because I'm finding out who I am.

And if I was a real wild animal
Then I'd have left by now.

I say
My brain isn't broken
It's like this for a reason
I'm like this for a reason
I'm becoming who I am.

And I'm scared
And you're scared
Because who I am might not be who you want me
to be.
Or who you are.

And I don't know why, but I *don't* say
It's all going to be okay.
There are so many things I stopped saying to you.

I want to say them
But I can't.

I pick up my plate
Put it in the kitchen
And go upstairs.

*The cast turn their placards over. The first word of
each is 'hello' or 'hi'.*
They start to drop them one by one.

SEGEN   Hey
          Mum
          I know I'm difficult
          But I don't mean to be
          I don't want to be the reason you're upset
          I want you to understand

I'm still your little girl
Just… older
I want you to accept I need space
I want to go to university outside London
Because I'm ready to leave home
I want us to be friends
I still need you.

GRACIA   Hello
I want to tell you something
That I've never told you
I want to say
Thank you
You light up my life
Everytime I get hurt
You have been my nurse
Even when you complain
Because I don't wear
Bright clothes
And don't do the dishes
We still laugh at the end
Sorry if I treated you badly
I love you.

MICHAEL   Hello
I want to ask you
Will you love me
No matter what I do?
It feels like…
You don't know who I am any more
I worry you've given up on me
What you think… that's not me
I am scared about the future
I think about us every night.

SERAFINA   Hello
I need to tell you
A couple of things
I could never say to you
So here goes…

I love you.
Always have, always will
I understand what it's like
From your point of view,
(Partly)
I know you're looking out for me
I know you care
I appreciate it
I am grateful.

DOYIN   Hello
I need to tell you something
You're the first person I talk to about anything
I adore your care
And support about my future
But sometimes you need to stop worrying
My future, I will figure it out later
I need to live my life as me
I do love you
I will be happy
And make you proud.

YAAMIN   Hey
Nothing can replace you
You're very important to me
I need you to know something
I need space!!!
…and so do you
I need you to know something
I need you!!
I love you.

TYREL   Hi
I need to tell you something
You are
The one who raised me
The one who helped me
You're always there
When I step through
The door

BUT
You worry too much
I do listen to you
When you tell me to focus on college
And not on girls
I know the rights and wrongs
I'll be fine
But please nag me less
About my chores!!

JACK   Hello
I need to tell you something
Sometimes
I need to do things on my own
I need to make my own decisions
I know that it's hard for you
But, you're going to have to get used to it
You need to let me go to parties
After all
You grew up in the seventies!!!
I do love you
Thank you
You've always helped me.

SAMA   Hey
I love you (a lot)
I always will but,
Sometimes you forget
I'm not my sister
…I'm not perfect
I never will be
I need you to be okay…
When I make mistakes
I know that me growing up
Is terrifying to you
But, I need you to know,
I'll be alright xxx.

NOAH   Hi
I've been meaning to say this for a while

THANKS
Thank you for the good
And the bad
Thank you for letting me play your guitar
Thanks for letting me play Amy Winehouse
Even though she's loud and rude
And talks about drugs all the time
Thank you for trying
Thanks for doing everything you could
And just like you said
Let's all walk off into the sun
Together
All five of us.

You Don't Know This Yet

The last placard is dropped. GRACIA *stands.*

GRACIA   Look at us.

> *She points at each cast member as she reintroduces them.*

> That's Segen.
> That's Yaamin.
> Doyin, Sama.
> Tyrel.
> Noah.
> Michael.
> Serafina.

> That's Jack. He's thirteen, he's the youngest one here.

> I'm Gracia. I'm eighteen, I'm the oldest one here.

> I remember when I was thirteen, I was like when I'm eighteen I'll be a real grown-up and I'll have my own flat and a job and loads of money and a really hot boyfriend and… actually I'm still doing the same things and I'm in my same bedroom with my sister and I totally don't feel like a grown-up, even though I officially am one.

> It's only five years ago but it seems like ages.

> And I don't know what happens next.

> But you do.

> Before the show, you wrote a message to your teenage self. Something you didn't know when you were our age. Do you remember?

> *A bucket containing the cards written by audience members is brought on to the stage. The cast, apart from* JACK *and* GRACIA, *take one each to read out.*

DOYIN   You don't know this yet, but...

NOAH   You don't know this yet, but...

SAMA   You don't know this yet, but...

TYREL   You don't know this yet, but...

MICHAEL   You don't know this yet, but...

SERAFINA   You don't know this yet, but...

SEGEN   You don't know this yet, but...

YAAMIN   You don't know this yet, but...

JACK   You don't know this yet.

GRACIA   But you will.

             Blackout.

BRAINSTORM

The Blueprint

Overview

Brainstorm is a play about teenage brain development, told through the real-life experiences of the young people who create and perform it. We've produced this blueprint because we want anyone to be able to make their own version.

The *Brainstorm* script is made up of two different types of content:

- *Scientific content* (information about the brain)
- *Personal content* (stories and experiences of the cast which make sense of the science)

If you want to perform your own version of *Brainstorm*, first contact Nick Hern Books (see details on page 2) to arrange a licence.

You will be provided with a template of the script in which you will find all the *scientific content* from the original script. Then use the blueprint which follows here to develop the *personal content* with your cast, incorporate it into the script template, and arrive at a complete script for your own production of *Brainstorm*.

You can choose to work through the blueprint scene by scene, or use it more freely as a source of inspiration and ideas.

Starting Out

We believe that young people have too many rules in their lives, so we only have three which are designed to ensure all our work is safe, fun and productive. They are:

- Be kind
- Be brave
- Be yourself

In addition, we found these three ideas useful when devising *Brainstorm*:

- Keep it contemporary – this is a play that is set right now, in the world and time the cast currently live in.

- Acknowledge your audience – don't pretend that they're not there.

- Vary the tone – be careful that it doesn't become too sentimental.

Using Personal Content

It is important to be sensitive and careful when using personal or autobiographical material in a play. Building the right atmosphere of safety, trust and support in which young people feel they can share is essential, and it is important to acknowledge with your cast from the very start that no one will be asked to share or perform anything that they don't feel comfortable with. Schools and youth groups should ensure that generating material is done in accordance with their own safeguarding policies.

Brainstorm is a play about brain development, but it's also about the impact that this has on teenagers' relationships with their parents. One of the main reasons teenagers' brains change is to enable them to become independent of their parents and this can place huge strain on these relationships. Parents should be made aware of the subject of the play from the start; and they should be told in advance that they are likely to appear as characters in some of the scenes.

Editing

As you create content, you'll find yourself having to make tough choices about what to include and what to leave out. Be brutal! Only include content that helps the audience understand the play and the things we need to know about the cast. Try not to say the same thing twice. It will help if you and the cast agree from the start that any content that you cut is about the play, rather than about them personally.

Casting

Our version of *Brainstorm* was made with ten teenagers, but you could make your version with anything from six upwards. The wider the age range, the better – our oldest was eighteen and the youngest was thirteen.

There are six key roles in the play. They carry the journey of the play and represent different elements within it. All other lines/actions can be carried out with any number of other performers. You may find that you can split some of the key roles between separate performers.

Oldest is the oldest person in the company. They start and finish the play.

Youngest gets teased for being the youngest person in the company.

Sprouting explains the process of learning in the teenage brain.

Pre-Frontal Cortex (PFC) impersonates their parent to demonstrate the 'sensible' part of the brain.

Conflict has an explosive fight with their parent that builds through the play.

Limbic makes everyone have fun and take risks.

In this blueprint and in the script template we have gendered these roles according to the original performers, but young people of any gender can play any of the roles.

The Science

The best way to understand the science in the play is to read the original *Brainstorm* script.

If you would like to do more research, there are hundreds of useful websites, articles, videos and podcasts online. We worked with leading adolescent neuroscientist Professor Sarah-Jayne Blakemore and we would recommend starting your research by looking up her excellent TED Talk, *The Mysterious Workings of the Adolescent Brain*.

The science is constantly developing, which is why we haven't included links here. Try and find the most up-to-date information.

It's really important that everyone in the cast understands the science: to introduce it use your research or extracts from the script template and ask the company to reinterpret it. They might, for example, build a set of neurons and synapses out of pencils and rubber bands, or create a dance representing the Limbic System.

Devising Exercises

As well as the specific exercises provided for each scene, the following exercises that we use a lot at Company Three might be useful.

Interviews and transcription

Interview the cast in small groups or one-to-one about their personal experiences of the ideas and themes in the play. Record the interviews and transcribe the most promising bits. Share and discuss.

Free writing

Set a starting point or topic and ask the cast to write freely in response, from their gut, without thinking about what they're writing and without stopping. It doesn't have to be neat, spelt right or make sense.

The cast can write paragraphs with prompts such as:

> I don't understand why…
> Being a teenager is…
> My brain feels like…

Or lists with specific titles such as:

> Things in my bedroom
> Things my mum says to me
> Questions I'd never ask my parents

Find interesting ways of getting the cast to share their writing back to the group.

Solo tasks

Ask your cast to take away an idea and to spend a short time creating a solo response to it. This helps to create personal material that isn't compromised by collaboration. The response could be some writing, a scene, a song, a picture, a challenge, a debate – anything.

Get out of the rehearsal room

Our best ideas often come when we least expect them. If you can, find time to hang out as a company in less formal settings: go outside, cook together, go on a trip, do something totally unrelated to the play.

The Set

Brainstorm can be performed with very little budget and with just a blank stage, if necessary.

We set our version of the play on a plain white platform surrounded by simple wooden furniture, representing a collage of different teenage bedrooms. The furniture contained hundreds of objects and items of clothing found in teenagers' bedrooms which were thrown all over the set before the Bedrooms scene.

The set included a wardrobe on which we projected the mobile-phone screen.

We strongly encourage you to come up with an original set design that works for your version of the play. If you choose to replicate our original design, please credit Charlie Damigos, the designer for the production.

Projection

A key part of our production was the ability to project a mobile-phone screen on to the wardrobe in the set. We connected an iPhone to an Apple TV box (this can be bought relatively cheaply or borrowed) and then fed the Apple TV through a projector.

For more information on how we used technology in *Brainstorm*, the National Theatre have made a short film about it which you can watch at www.companythree.co.uk/brainstorm.

More Information

For more information about our version of *Brainstorm*, including videos, photos, resources, reviews, go to www.companythree.co.uk/brainstorm.

Contact Us

We'd love to hear about your journey as you make your own *Brainstorm*. Please feel free to share your process, photos and thoughts with us:

Email hello@companythree.co.uk
Twitter @company_three
Instagram @companythree

Scene by Scene

Over the next few pages you'll find a simple overview of each scene in the play, followed by practical exercises you can use to generate and write the personal content with your cast. This can then be added into the script template.

Before the Show

As the audience arrives they are given postcards on which they are asked to write a message to their teenage self, starting with the words 'You don't know this yet but…'

These are collected up and a small number selected to be read out in the final scene of the play.

Scene 1: Introduction

Oldest introduces the play and the basics of teenage brain development. Her monologue is interspersed with the arrival onstage of the other cast members – in ascending age order.

As each new person enters, Oldest tells us their name, their age and a fact or two about them. When the person playing Limbic enters, they might do something naughty or unexpected.

Sourcing the facts for the introductions

- Ask your cast to introduce themselves to the group then introduce someone else to the group.

- Ask the cast to write facts about themselves then ask everyone to guess whose is whose.

Select the facts which help to seed themes and stories that emerge later in the play, e.g. puberty, growing up, interaction with parents (Parent Duologues), our relationship with our phones, learning, school.

The facts should be a mixture of fun, funny and personal. They should feel very current – they could even be changed every night. There may be moments of short (scripted) dialogue or response from other cast members.

Scene 2: Bedrooms

The cast members describe their bedrooms to us in a series of short monologues. The scene is divided into three sections:

A: Messy Bedrooms
B: Private Space
C: Bedrooms and Phones

The monologues are interrupted intermittently by parents calling to get the cast's attention. In one of these interruptions we see the start of Conflict's argument with his parent which builds through the play (see Parent Duologues and Stand-off).

Generating material for the monologues

- Ask your cast to record a video tour of their bedroom and share it with everyone else in rehearsal.

- Ask the cast to imagine their bedrooms in the rehearsal room and take one another on a tour.

- Ask the cast to free-write lists using titles such as 'objects in my bedroom', 'things my parents know/don't know about my bedroom', 'things my parents like/don't like about my bedroom'.

Scene 3: Sprouting

Sprouting describes why the teenage brain is so good at learning and how some parts of it develop quicker than others. The cast each demonstrate a skill via a YouTube tutorial.

Creating the YouTube tutorials

- Ask the cast to share YouTube tutorials they watch or have made in the past – what are the common features? What makes a great video?

- Set everyone the task of filming their own YouTube tutorial at home and share them with the group in rehearsal.

Select key lines from each tutorial to insert into the script. The tutorials should reflect a range of interests and ways of learning.

Scene 4: Pre-Frontal Cortex

The cast explain that the Pre-Frontal Cortex (PFC) is the 'sensible' part of the brain that's a bit like your dad (or mum). The cast become their parents by putting on an item of their clothing. They introduce themselves to the audience by telling us their name, who their child is and a fact or two about themselves. They end up having a dance party until PFC's parent stops the fun.

Building the characters of the parents

- Ask the cast to do an observation exercise on their parents and record their findings to share back with the group.

- Run a drama workshop with the cast in role as their parents – how does each parent introduce themselves? How do they respond to the exercises?

- Run a series of improvisations with the parents in which they have to dance (e.g. a wedding, dance class, in private at home).

- Collect a list of parents' favourite dancing songs – choose one to play into the scene for them all to dance to.

Select facts for each parent to use as their introduction. The focus of this scene should be on presenting accurate (and loving) portrayals of the parents, not mocking impersonations. The facts that the parents tell us could reflect their relationship with their child, their hobbies, their favourite things, etc.

Scene 5: Parent Duologues

The cast recreate key arguments and conversations they have had with their parents. This includes Conflict's argument with his parent that continues to build during the play.

Generating content for the arguments/conversations

- Talk about different conversations the cast have had with their parents when they have misunderstood each other.

- Make a list of things the cast's parents want them to do which they don't want to do.

- Ask the cast to look back through text-message conversations they've had with their parents.

Creating short duologues

- Ask the cast to write duologues using this content with different word restrictions (e.g a six-word scene, a two-line scene, a six-line scene, a ten-line scene). Focus on what each character wants.

- Ask the cast to improvise/perform these scenes:
  – Direct other people as the parent and yourself.
  – Play your own parent and have someone else play you.
  – Play yourself and have someone else play your parent.

The scenes you select should be a mix of angry, tender and funny. They should be varying lengths – some may be only a few lines long. In this scene each cast member should play themselves, with other cast members playing their parent. Some duologues could be delivered on the phone or by text message.

You might want to include the following 'types' of conflict to ensure a good spread of content:

– A parent wants help with technology.
– A parent wants to know how school/exams are going.
– A cast member wants to stay out late.
– A cast member refuses to come out of their room.
– A parent wants their child to confide in them as a friend.

Scene 6: Brain Scan

The cast take part in an anonymous survey revealing things about themselves that they would rather not reveal publicly and giving an insight into the deepest parts of their brain.

The survey takes the form of first person statements (e.g. 'I lied to my parents today', 'Sex scares me') that the cast answer 'yes' or 'no' to.

Generating content for the statements

• Ask the cast's parents to fill in an anonymous form sharing what they'd like to know about their children's lives.

• Ask the cast to write possible questions on pieces of paper that are then screwed up, shared and read out anonymously.

• Ask the cast to write down secrets anonymously and turn these into statements.

Making the survey

• There are lots of ways to do this: challenge the cast to come up with ways to answer questions (you can use practice questions if you like) without revealing who has answered what.

• We used ten bedroom lamps with long dimmer cables bought from Ikea. We tangled the cables up, gave each cast member a switch and instructed them to turn their lamp on for 'yes' and lamps off for 'no'. The questions were projected on to the set but could also be read out live. We didn't change the questions every night, but you could do.

Scene 7: Limbic System

Youngest and Limbic tell us about the limbic system. Limbic interrupts Youngest's monologue and takes control of the play. He gets the audience involved in a rowdy game of 'Never Have I Ever' and then leads the cast into a wild party.

During the party, Conflict is distracted, thinking back to the argument he had earlier on in Parent Duologues (he might receive a phone call or text which triggers this). He becomes more and more agitated and eventually explodes in an angry outburst.

Generating statements for 'Never Have I Ever'

- Ask the cast to share the most dangerous/stupid/naughty/ risky things they (or their friends) have ever done. This can be done anonymously by writing on pieces of paper and throwing them into a hat.
- Play 'Never Have I Ever' as a company (be careful!).

Making the party:

- Ask the cast to create tableaux of typical wild parties/ raves that they have experienced or heard about. Use these to define choreography and events that take place during a party.

- As a company, plot the story of how the party unfolds (particularly charting Conflict's journey within it) and then loses control. A simple structure might be:

  1. Getting ready (while Limbic talks)
  2. Dancing
  3. Breaking the rules (pillow fights, pranking, throwing sweets)
  4. Going too far (things start to get out of hand)
  5. Conflict loses it – angry explosion

Scene 8: Stand-off

Conflict loses control and shouts as if at his parent in the climax of an argument. Everyone shuts themselves in their rooms in a strop. One parent gently pleads with their child, who starts to tidy up. Another cast member tries to explain to their parent why they are the way they are.

Generating content for Conflict's monologue

- Ask the cast member playing Conflict to chart a real argument that they've had with one of their parents. Break it down into scenes or moments – build up, climax, consequence.

- Ask them to free-write as a stream of consciousness all the things they felt in the climax of this argument. These might be things they did say, or never said.

- Ask them to create physical expressions of their emotions in the climax of the argument.

- Pair another cast member with Conflict in the role of his parent so that they can improvise both sides of the argument as it climaxes. Then take away the parent's voice.

Generating content for the 'Because…' monologue

- Ask the cast to free-write a list of all the things their parents say to them all the time.

- Ask the cast to write the question 'Why am I like this?' at the top of a piece of paper and write a list of answers that begin with the word 'because…'

When constructing the final monologue you might choose to use one person's response or an amalgamation of lots of responses.

We used 'Cups (You're Gonna Miss Me When I'm Gone)' sung live by one of the cast members to underscore part of this section. This was suggested by a cast member. If you'd like to use singing, find something that is relevant to this moment in the play and to your cast.

Scene 9: Risks

The cast members are still isolated, shut up in their rooms.
They communicate without physically speaking to the audience
(e.g. via projected WhatsApp messages), explaining that the
combination of all the messy changes happening in their brains
fills them with huge potential. They share examples of positive
risk-taking to demonstrate this.

Generating the list of risks

- Have a discussion about teenagers who have changed the
  world – insert these into the explanation.

- Ask the cast to share personal examples of positive risks
  that they have taken – moments where they have had to
  be particularly brave, stepped outside their comfort zone
  or done something significant for the first time.

- If you cannot project phones on stage, experiment with
  different ways of communicating the lines in the scene
  without speaking.

Scene 10: You Say to Me, I Say to You

Conflict delivers a monologue to his parent explaining how he
feels about his brain and the changes he is going through.
The rest of the cast show placards written specifically for their
parents which express things they want to say to them but can't.

Generating content for the placards

- Ask the cast to write a personal letter to one of their
  parents. Work one-to-one with each cast member to
  understand what the most important phrases and
  sentiments are within the letter. Divide these into
  a series of short sentences (one phrase per placard) over
  approximately ten placards each.

The content should be honest, tender and funny without being
overly sentimental.

Scene 11: You Don't Know This Yet

Oldest reintroduces the cast by name. She delivers a short monologue contrasting what she knows about her past, her present and her future. The cast read out the some of the 'You don't know this yet but...' postcards that the audience filled out before the play started. This reconnects the audience to their teenage selves and to the teenagers on stage.

Generating content for the monologue

- Ask the cast to write a description of what their life will be like when they're eighteen. Share these and discuss them.

- Ask the rest of the cast to interview the cast member playing Oldest about how they imagined their life would be at their current age when they were thirteen and how different the reality is, e.g. they thought they'd have their own flat but they're still living with their mum.

Other Plays for Young People to Perform from Nick Hern Books

Original Plays

100
Christopher Heimann,
Neil Monaghan, Diene Petterle

BANANA BOYS
Evan Placey

BLOOD AND ICE
Liz Lochhead

BOYS
Ella Hickson

BUNNY
Jack Thorne

BURYING YOUR BROTHER IN THE PAVEMENT
Jack Thorne

CHRISTMAS IS MILES AWAY
Chloë Moss

COCKROACH
Sam Holcroft

DISCO PIGS
Enda Walsh

EIGHT
Ella Hickson

THE FALL
James Fritz

GIRLS LIKE THAT
Evan Placey

HOLLOWAY JONES
Evan Placey

I CAUGHT CRABS IN WALBERSWICK
Joel Horwood

MOGADISHU
Vivienne Franzmann

MOTH
Declan Greene

THE MYSTAE
Nick Whitby

OVERSPILL
Ali Taylor

PRONOUN
Evan Placey

SAME
Deborah Bruce

THERE IS A WAR
Tom Basden

THE URBAN GIRL'S GUIDE TO CAMPING AND OTHER PLAYS
Fin Kennedy

THE WARDROBE
Sam Holcroft

Adaptations

ANIMAL FARM
Ian Wooldridge
Adapted from George Orwell

ARABIAN NIGHTS
Dominic Cooke

BEAUTY AND THE BEAST
Laurence Boswell

CORAM BOY
Helen Edmundson
Adapted from Jamila Gavin

DAVID COPPERFIELD
Alastair Cording
Adapted from Charles Dickens

GREAT EXPECTATIONS
Nick Ormerod and Declan Donnellan
Adapted from Charles Dickens

HIS DARK MATERIALS
Nicholas Wright
Adapted from Philip Pullman

THE JUNGLE BOOK
Stuart Paterson
Adapted from Rudyard Kipling

KENSUKE'S KINGDOM
Stuart Paterson
Adapted from Michael Morpurgo

KES
Lawrence Till
Adapted from Barry Hines

NOUGHTS & CROSSES
Dominic Cooke
Adapted from Malorie Blackman

THE RAILWAY CHILDREN
Mike Kenny
Adapted from E. Nesbit

SWALLOWS AND AMAZONS
Helen Edmundson and Neil Hannon
Adapted from Arthur Ransome

TO SIR, WITH LOVE
Ayub Khan-Din
Adapted from E.R Braithwaite

TREASURE ISLAND
Stuart Paterson
Adapted from Robert Louis Stevenson

WENDY & PETER PAN
Ella Hickson
Adapted from J.M. Barrie

THE WOLVES OF WILLOUGHBY CHASE
Russ Tunney
Adapted from Joan Aiken

For more information on plays to perform visit
www.nickhernbooks.co.uk/plays-to-perform